Parables of Cakes

Responding to God's
unique love and call in our lives

Ayoma Fonseka

FriesenPress

Suite 300 - 990 Fort St
Victoria, BC, V8V 3K2
Canada

www.friesenpress.com

Copyright © 2016 by Ayoma Fonseka
First Edition — 2016

Photographer : Steven Elphick
Foreword: Rev. Fr. Thomas Rosica, CSB

All cakes are designed and created by Ayoma of Ayoma Cake Masterpieces (http://www.ayomacakes.com) and photographed by courtsy of Steve (Steven Elphick Photography); except the image of my hands in the chapter 'Surrender'.

Visions and messages shared in this book are entirely my personal experiences. They are shared to inspire the reader - that God communicates with all His children.

All rights reserved.

No part of this publication may be reproduced in any form, or by any means, electronic or mechanical, including photocopying, recording, or any information browsing, storage, or retrieval system, without permission in writing from FriesenPress.

ISBN
978-1-4602-9501-4 (Paperback)

1. RELIGION, CHRISTIAN THEOLOGY, SOTERIOLOGY

Distributed to the trade by The Ingram Book Company

Unless otherwise indicated, all scripture references are taken from the Revised Standard Version of the Bible, copyright 1952 [2nd edition, 1971] by the Division of Christian Education of the National Council of the Churches of Christ in the United States of America. Used by permission. All rights reserved.

Scripture references marked (NIV) are taken from the Holy Bible, NEW INTERNATIONAL VERSION®. Copyright © 1973, 1978, 1984, 2011 by Biblica, Inc. All rights reserved worldwide. Used by permission. NEW INTERNATIONAL VERSION® and NIV® are registered trademarks of Biblica, Inc. Use of either trademark for the offering of goods or services requires the prior written consent of Biblica US, Inc.

Table of Contents

Dedication	vi
Thank You	1
Foreward	3
Chosen by God	7
God is Love	13
God in the Centre	19
Surrender	25
True Confession	31
Forgiveness	37
Bride of Christ	43
An Invitation	49

Dedication

This book is dedicated to my (late) amazing, beloved mother, Hema Karunaratne – who did not get the opportunity to see the completion of the book.

And
To
Trevins, Treyomi & Trehani Fonseka

And
To all my cake decorating instructors from around the world!

Thank You

Thank You, **Holy Spirit** for the gift of creativity and inspiration!

Thank you, **Fr. Thomas Rosica** for the 'Forward' and reading the manuscript at the airport.

Thank you **Dr. Irene D Souza** for the book title

Thank you, **Fr. Roger Vandenakker** for the subtitle.

Thank you, my former **spiritual director** for leading me to the Lord.

Thank you, **Steve Elphick** for all the beautiful photographs - a generous gift. I appreciate numerous weekends you and **Paula Elphick** spent at the studio photographing all the cakes. Thank you for sacrificing your time and talent.

Thank you, **Rosemary Elstone** and **Donann Schloss** for all the endless hours you both spent editing the manuscript.

Thank you **Mary Brown** for proof reading the manuscript

Photography – courtesy of Steve Elphick of Steve Elphick Photography, Toronto

May the Lord bless every one of you for the generous gift of your time and talent!

IT IS A PLEASURE FOR ME TO WRITE SOME WORDS OF introduction to Ayoma's reflections on the daily living of the Christian faith. Ayoma leads us all on a journey through her profession of baker and cake maker, reminding us that the Lord speaks to us in the ordinary daily activities of our life, through our relationships, friendships, and all the high and low moments of our life.

As I read her pages, the thought this thought remains: "We are called to find God in all people and in all things." It is clear that Ayoma loves the Word of God and allows her life to be inspired by that Word. She also sees her life through the lenses of Scripture and offers us a model of discernment of the Lord's presence in the ordinary. For Ayoma, the Christian faith is a mystery that we experience each day. She stresses the importance of Spiritual Direction, Sacramental Confession, Reception of the Eucharist which is her true food, and daily prayer. Ayoma's faith is contagious and spreads to all those who come in contact with her. She is living proof that when we allow the Lord into our lives, he makes a masterpiece out of what we thought to be so small and insignificant.

"May the Lord bless Ayoma and help her to cook up a storm, making wonderful specialty cakes as she encourages many others to draw closer to the Lord of the Church."

Fr. Thomas Rosica, CSB
CEO, Salt and Light Catholic Media Foundation
Christmas 2013

Chosen by God

You did not choose me but I chose you.
(John 15:16, NRSV)

AS A CONVERT FROM BUDDHISM TO CHRISTIANITY, I STRUG-gled with the verse of Scripture: *"You did not choose me but I chose you,"* (John 15:16). If God chose to have a relationship with everyone and died for all (2 Corinthians 5:15), how is it that all do not follow Jesus? Did He choose only certain people? Why was I born into a Buddhist family? Why are there various faiths or religions? Why are there fallen Christians? Why are there several denominations among Christians? All these questions lingered in my mind for years. Subsequently, I realized that I was not alone; many of my Christian friends in the Roman Catholic Church have pondered the same questions.

The Lord, in His goodness, answered my questions in great detail. Surprisingly, He asked me to reflect on a cake decorating class I had taught in 2007. Over the years I had taught many cake decorating classes to hundreds of students at a culinary college in Toronto, yet He drew my attention to that specific class. The Lord requested that I pay attention to every step and every detail of this class, from the beginning to the end. Although I had no idea why that particular class was significant, I obeyed the Lord and ruminated over all the details. It was easy for me to revisit every aspect of this class. For some reason, it has remained etched in my memory for all these years.

I pondered the details of that class. It was a beginner's class for basic decorating—the stepping stone into the world of cake decorating. As usual, the class was advertised months in advance in the college calendar, through brochures, by word-of-mouth, and on social media. Generally, all cake decorating classes are filled to capacity, and at times a second class is added to accommodate the overflow. However, this particular class didn't have a full enrollment, which was unusual. Instead of cancelling it altogether, though, we commenced on the scheduled night with fewer participants.

On the first night of the class, I arrived early to make preparations. It was my responsibility to ensure that all necessary ingredients and equipment were available and in their proper places prior to the arrival of the students. The students arrived, and I marked attendance. At that point, everyone gathered around my workstation to observe my demonstration of the basic piping designs while I described the specific technique I was using. The students then returned to their workstations to begin piping. While they practiced, I approached them individually to answer questions and to offer any needed guidance and assistance. Some students worked with great enthusiasm, a few had some difficulty, and others struggled to understand and master the new skill I'd taught them. For those who were struggling, I offered to guide their hands to help them achieve the desired results.

This was a weekly class, and by the third week I observed that some students had already dropped out. Interestingly, even among those who decided to persevere until the end of the course, there were some who chose not to continue to the next level. I surmised that some students were probably not prepared to make the necessary sacrifices that learning a new skill involves: sacrifices of time, effort, patience, and endurance.

After reviewing the events and experiences of the cake decorating class, the astounding similarities between John 15:16 and the class became evident to me. The course description of the cake decorating class was made available through various information channels, but it appealed only to a few. Among those who became aware of the class, only a few chose to enroll. Similarly, all are called by God, and His

Word is available to all mankind, yet only some choose to receive the teachings of Jesus Christ and to pursue His path. Others opt to belong to a different religious faith or spiritual orientation, while some reject the path of faith altogether. Here we see the exercise of our God-given gift of free will. God doesn't deprive us of choice, even if that choice is not to follow Him or know Him.

Some of those who have decided to follow Jesus after hearing the Gospel will eventually quit, fall away, or become discouraged when the level of commitment and hard work present too great a challenge or a seemingly insurmountable obstacle. Like some of my students, these people may find the teachings of God to be too demanding. Lacking patience and endurance, they give up the struggle.

God never claimed that following Him would be easy. Instead, He described it as a narrow path that only a few would choose to accept. The teachings of Jesus indicate that the life of His followers would be filled not only with blessings, but also with trials and tribulations. Nevertheless, He promised to be with us in the midst of our difficulties. He helps us, much like the instructor who guides the hand of the student. In His words, even if we are abandoned by our own mothers, He will never abandon us (Isaiah 49:15).

A cake designer, like any professional in any field, has to strive constantly to learn more, hone and improve skills, and move ahead in artistry in order to reach maximum potential. It's a similar situation when one follows Jesus. Our final aim as believing, practicing Christians is to be with our loving Father in Heaven. We must direct our learning and efforts towards that goal, all the while building His Kingdom here on Earth.

In a life full of difficulties, Jesus is the answer. Whenever we struggle with the difficulties and disappointments of life, it's a sweet consolation to be able to lean on our Almighty God for assistance and guidance; on our own, we are helpless.

It wasn't my choice to be born a Buddhist; the choice to follow Buddhism was made by my parents. However, it was my choice to remain a Buddhist or to convert to Christianity and follow Jesus.

God's answer to my questions was revealed to me through the decorating class of 2007. It served as a catalyst by providing me with a simple answer to a complex question: If all are called or chosen by God, why do only a few follow Him? The answer, I came to discover, is our free will (Revelation 3:20).

God is Love

I have loved you with an everlasting love; therefore I have continued my faithfulness to you. (Jeremiah 31:3, NRSV)

LOVE—THE EPITOME OF LOVE IS EXPRESSED THROUGH THE suffering and death of Jesus Christ on the cross. There is no love greater than the love of God. Although we can verbalize God's love for all mankind, His real love must be experienced to be fully understood.

In Ephesians 3:18, St. Paul writes that he prays that God's people will have the power to comprehend the breadth and length and height and depth of God's love for them. In our human intelligence, however, we lack the capacity to fully fathom the magnanimity of God's love for us. Whether we are cognizant of it or not, we experience a glimpse of God's love, and have the opportunity to express His love daily, through our interactions with one another. It's God's love within us that enables us to extend ourselves to others, whether they are family, friends, acquaintances, or strangers. For those we love, we make numerous sacrifices to let them know they are loved. We sacrifice our time and re-organize our schedules to accommodate their needs, even when we don't feel like doing so. We're constantly extending ourselves to accommodate the needs of those we love by placing their needs before our own. Any action we perform in love is an expression of, and an experience of, God's love. Without His love in our hearts, we are incapable of extending genuine love to others.

God's love for His children is unconditional and immeasurable. To exemplify His deep, abiding love, God directed my attention to the process of creating a custom cake. Each custom cake is a unique, one-of-a-kind work of art designed and created with love, passion, and enthusiasm. Its creation begins with a sketch of the artist's vision and a plan for the completion of that vision. From the sketch to the masterpiece, there are various intermediate steps that require hard work and long hours. The creative process calls for a special level of commitment and attention to detail from the artist. It's the love for the project that enables the designer to spend numerous hours designing, baking, and decorating a cake. At times, one has to sacrifice sleep in order to work all night to meet a deadline. Successfully completing the project requires knowledge and decorating skills, together with diligence, endurance, energy, perseverance, determination, and the ability to pay attention to every minute detail of design.

Ultimately, the driving forces behind this type of project are LOVE and passion. If either characteristic is lacking during the process of creation, it becomes mentally and physically difficult to maintain momentum and continue the work to its completion. A lack of these important qualities would be reflected in the finished product. Without these key elements, the cake would be an ordinary cake instead of a vision of beauty. On the other hand, if the cake is completed with an outpouring of one's heart and soul, the artist is able to step back and appreciate the beauty of the completed workmanship—an edible masterpiece.

Similarly, we are God's masterpiece. We are uniquely designed and created by Him in His image and in His likeness. He doesn't take the "cookie-cutter" approach to His creations. We are not mass produced. He has made us all unique, according to His custom design. He has created every individual with great care and immense love, attending to every minute aspect and detail. Like the cake designer, He sees the beauty in each creation; He is the Divine Creator. Each person is precious to Him. Each person is His masterpiece—designed and created in His LOVE.

A simple prayer was given to me by the Lord in 2009: Lord, help me today to walk in the path of your light, in the path of your love, and in the path of your peace. Amen!

God in the Centre

He himself is before all things, and in him all things hold together. (Colossians 1:17, NRSV)

SCRIPTURE CLEARLY STATES THAT GOD HOLDS ALL THINGS together. This powerful message is illustrated through a multi-tiered cake. The design and the composition of this cake emphasize two other significant messages: the need for unity among all God's children, and the preciousness of each person in our Creator's eyes.

I was always encouraged by my spiritual director to have my eyes fixed on Jesus. This cake exemplifies his advice. In this configuration, the bottom tier is shaped as a large blossom, while the rest of the tiers are round. Each tier is a different size and height. The tiers are held together by a strong centre pole, which is not visible. It's imperative that the centre pole be sturdy, as the strength of the pole provides the necessary support preventing the cakes from tumbling down/falling apart.

Similarly, though God cannot be seen, He is within each of us. When we make God the centre of our lives, we have a solid support holding us up when the storms of life come against us. He is our strength, and we are supported by Him (Ephesians 6:10).

No human can evade pain and suffering in life. We are faced daily with obstacles and struggles, but when God is in the centre of our lives, we aren't crushed beneath our burdens. Instead, when we turn to Him with our problems and conflicts we can find strength in God and in His promises.. Our God is not only a loving Father who promised never to abandon us (Isaiah 49:15), but He is also a God who chose and chooses to live and walk among us (Galatians 2:20).

God cares for us, and He will be always with us (Isaiah 46:4), even if at times we cease to feel His presence. He never promised us a life without struggles and difficulties, but He did say that in the world we would have tribulation, trials, and distress (John 16:33). Yet He promised that if we invite Him into the midst of our lives, giving Him control, He would help us to bear our difficulties for His glory. If we need support during times of adversity, God must be the centre of our lives.

Personally, I am blessed to be a Christian of the Roman Catholic tradition. As a Buddhist, I lacked the internal support on which I now rely. I had no one to turn to when faced with difficult situations, and no one to help me overcome life's obstacles. Now I have Jesus, the Almighty God.

Using the cake as a symbol, the Lord next wanted to highlight the importance of unity among all His children—His creations. Regardless of their different sizes, shapes, and colour, and in spite of varying workmanship, each cake is uniquely designed. Although each tier is different in its appearance with individualistic and unique elements, when assembled together they combine into a single unit of harmony, beauty, and majesty that provides great joy to the cake's creator.

Just as the cake tiers are different, every child of God is uniquely created by the Father. Regardless of colour, nationality, size, shape, or any other differences, we are all one in the eyes of the Creator. When all of God's children unite in solidarity as one family, it brings much glory and joy to our Creator, God the Father. We are all different, yet those differences are erased in Christ Jesus (Galatians 3:28).

Finally, this cake expresses the value God places on each of us—His cherished and precious children. The jewels on the cake represent each of His children. We are precious to Him.

A message given to me in a dream by our Lord: You are a child of the Most High God, and you are of utmost value to Him. He is the Creator, the Giver, the Author, and the Finisher of your life. Do not permit another human to place a value on you (cf. Romans 8:16).

Surrender

Humble yourselves before the Lord, and he will exalt you. (James 4:10, NRSV)

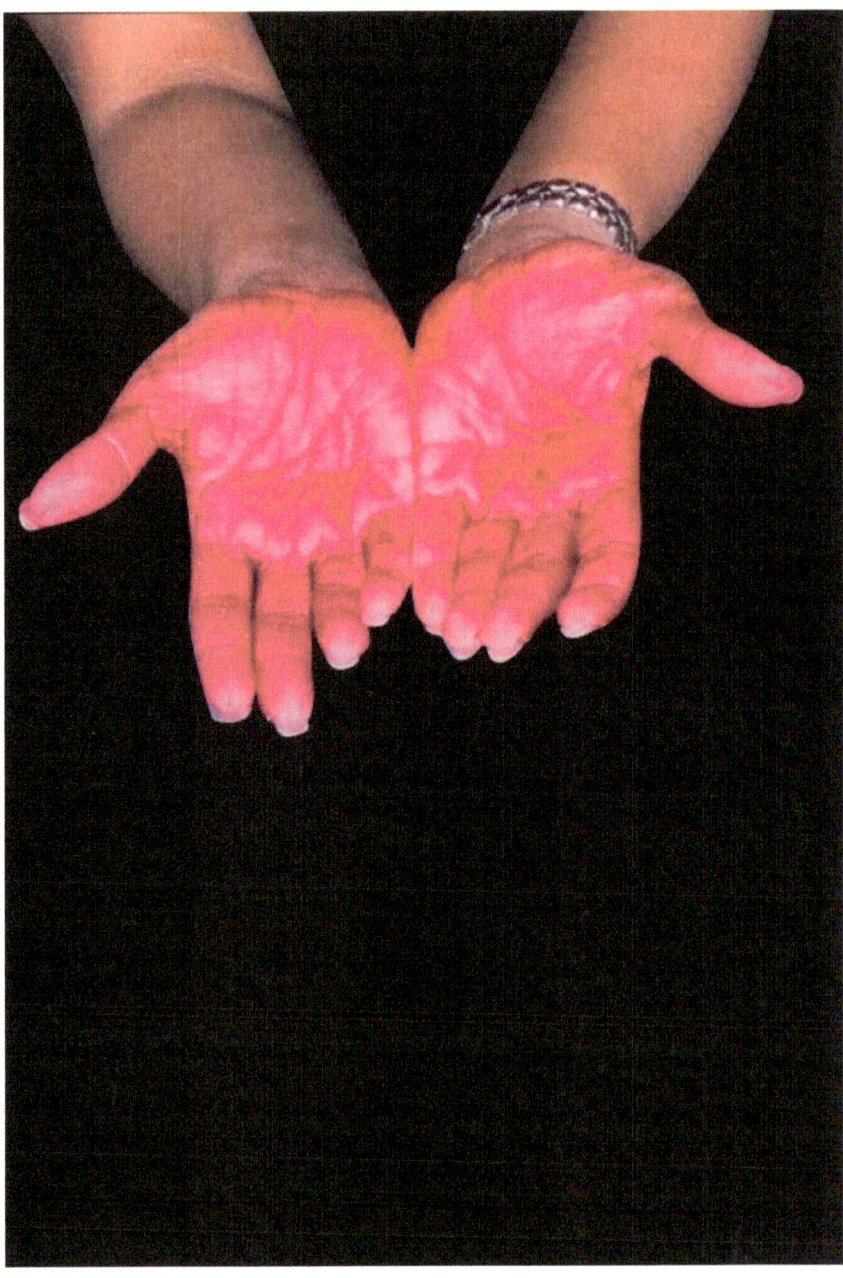

IT WAS THE SPRING OF 2007, THE YEAR I TRULY EMBRACED the Lord. I was meeting with a client to finalize the details of a cake and to sign the contract. Just prior to the meeting, it suddenly occurred to me that the cake was due on Holy Saturday. I was faced with a dilemma. It was too late to cancel the meeting, so I surrendered the entire situation to the Lord for His resolution. I said a quick prayer, asking the Lord to either take the order away from me, or use it to glorify Him.

I met with the client, discussed details of the cake, and we signed the contract. After the client's departure, I was filled with anxiety. I thought of the numerous hours required to complete the cake and wondered how I could get my work accomplished prior to the Good Friday service. I had completely forgotten Thursday evening Mass, the Last Supper of our Lord, which meant more hours spent in church and less spent on the cake. Nevertheless, I attended Thursday evening Mass, and after arriving home from church, I worked on the cake throughout the night and well into the following day.

Just prior to the Good Friday service, in order to complete the final decorations on the cake, I needed to prepare some red icing. In the back of my mind, I was wondering how the Lord intended to use this cake for His glory. I opened the bottle of red colouring to begin my task, when I realized it was almost time to attend church. I immediately closed the lid of the bottle and placed my hands under a running tap to rinse off the tiny bit of red colouring that streaked my fingertip. To my amazement, instead of the colour being washed off under the running water, it was running down my fingers, spreading across my hands, and completely covering both of my palms in red.

I was speechless, unable to comprehend what had occurred. The more I tried to wash off, the deeper the colour became. I found this rather surprising, as this had never happened to me before. I'd used red colouring in cakes for decades without significant staining to my hands. Nevertheless, as the time was rapidly approaching for the service, I wiped my still-red hands and left for church.

At the church, I followed the service with great intensity, paying no attention to my red-covered hands. Soon after the service ended, however, the two ladies sitting on either side of me inquired about what had happened to my hands to make them red, commenting that it looked as though my hands were bleeding. I responded that I had no explanation, as I'd never in the past experienced any similar occurrence. They both shared that my red-coloured hands had enabled them to focus on the wounds of Jesus and that, as a result, His suffering had become more real to both of them.

After arriving home, I washed my hands again to try to remove the colour, but with no success. This baffled me. Regardless of the continual washing of my hands, the bright red stain lasted until Easter, and then it disappeared.

I remained curious about what had caused my hands to be stained so completely red. Eventually, the Lord reminded me of my request that the cake be used for His glory. Because I accepted the cake order through obedience, He was able to use my hands as instruments to bring awareness of His painful crucifixion to two of His children, enabling them to recognize His suffering.

I am grateful to God for this unique experience. In all my years of cake decorating, such an event had never happened to me before, nor has it happened since.

I will share a prayer the Lord gave me in 2011: Lord, help me today to walk in humility, knowing you are God. Holy Spirit, take complete charge of my life and grant me the grace to surrender to your Holy will.

True Confession

… though your *sins* are like *scarlet*, they shall be as *white as snow*… (Isaiah 1:18, NRSV, emphasis added)

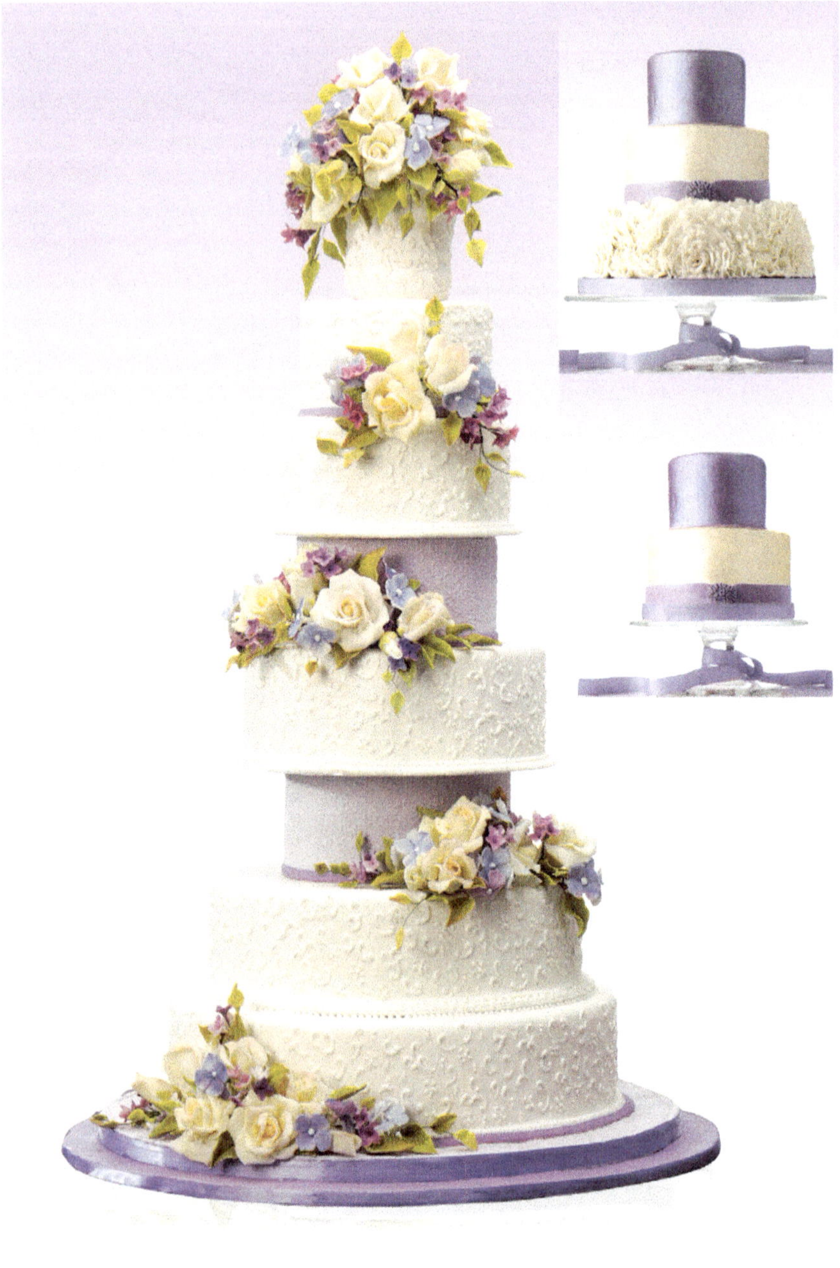

I WAS IN DEEP CONTEMPLATION, ALMOST IN A STATE OF sleep, when in a vision I saw three cakes: a cake with simple decoration, another with more advanced decoration, and an elaborate third cake with many hand sculpted sugar flowers and other decorative details. The creation of each of these cakes requires a different set of artistic skills. I wondered what this vision meant. The Lord responded that the cakes represent the three levels of confession. I was perplexed by this revelation and waited for further clarification from the Lord. His explanation changed my view of confession.

The two tier cake is simple in its appearance, indicating little time or planning was invested in its creation. This cake represents a quick, shallow confession made without fully engaging the heart and mind, or without spending much time or effort on self-examination and planning. This confession is made only through a sense of obligation as required by the church.

The second cake is an illustration of selective confession. It exhibits more workmanship and design. More time, effort, and thought was expended in its composition. However, the design is restricted by choice. Similarly, in selective confession, the penitent chooses which sins to reveal or acknowledge. All sins are not confessed, or conversely the seriousness of the offences is withheld from the confessor.

The elaborate cake has many tiers. Decorating each tier with icing details and hand crafting sugar flowers require time, effort, thought, and precision. It's this type of true confession the Lord expects from us—careful, thoughtful, precise, and complete.

Each tier of the cake is symbolic of an area in an individual's life. The Lord wants us to examine every area of our lives— our behaviours, our thoughts, our attitudes, and our treatment of others—in great detail. A confession made in accordance with church guidelines is a thorough examination of conscience in which one reviews and examines all sins with an aim of achieving a spirit of genuine repentance.

The repentant person must be well prepared before meeting with the priest in order to make a true, complete, and heartfelt confession. One's disposition toward confession is of utmost importance. The penitent must be truly sorry for having offended God and causing Him grief. He or she must approach the confessor and the confessional with the intention of making reparation for sins committed and changing his or her mind and behaviour by turning away from sin and becoming a godly person.

The Word of God says that the righteous man falls seven times and rises again (Proverbs 24:16). It doesn't grant permission to repeatedly indulge in the same sins. It's crucial to be aware that lifelong sinful habits cannot be changed quickly or by one visit to the confessional; however, all sins can be overcome with the help and grace of God. Mastery over sin is a gradual process. We are all sinners. If we say we are without sin, we deceive ourselves (1 John 1:8). In Sirach 4:26, it is written, *"Do not be ashamed to confess your sin …"* Without confession and the practice of regular self-examination, it's easy to remain stuck in habitual sin.

To stress the importance of a complete confession, the Lord gave me the following message: My children, what I desire from you is a true confession from the heart. Look into your heart and dig deep. Confess everything and do not hold back (Proverbs 28:13). Before approaching your confessor, prepare yourself by making every effort to examine your conscience honestly. You know I forgive all sins, big or small, yet it hurts me to witness my children holding back. Each tier of the cake represents an area of your life. Focus on each area of your life and examine it in great detail prior to confession. As you confess your sins, you will be blessed with much grace. Do not be afraid to come to me with an open heart. I am your loving Father who forgives even the smallest sin (1 John 1:9). My children, I love you (Romans 5:8).

Through the vision revealed to me, the Lord's message to all His children is very clear. He expects a true, complete, heartfelt confession of our sin(s) and not a partial or superficial admission of our faults or shortcomings. Confessing sin(s) to a priest (Leviticus 5: 5–6, Luke 5:24) is not practiced by all Christians. Many believers utilize other forms of confession mentioned in the Bible (James 5:16, Psalm 32:5). Nevertheless, the message is universal. God wants the entire truth confessed, as He is all Truth!

Forgiveness

So also my heavenly Father will do to every one of you, if you do not forgive your brother or sister from your heart. (Matthew 18:35, NRSV)

IN MICAH 7:18, IT IS WRITTEN THAT OUR GOD PARDONS SIN and forgives transgressions. He doesn't stay angry forever, but He delights in showing us mercy. Yet as followers of Christ, we struggle to forgive those who have wronged us, whether through simple misunderstandings or grave injustices. Sometimes we hold long-standing grudges against others. Nevertheless, the Lord commands us to forgive the wrongs done to us, whether trivial or serious, not once, but seventy times seven (Matthew 18:22). In other words, endlessly.

There is tremendous power in forgiveness and in praying for those who hurt us. One example in the Roman Catholic tradition is the story of St. Maria Goretti (October 16, 1890–July 6, 1902). Maria, an eleven-year-old peasant girl, died of multiple stab wounds inflicted by a neighbour (Alessandro) who attempted to rape her when she refused to submit to him. During her twenty painful hours of suffering, she prayed for and forgave Alessandro. After serving his prison sentence, Alessandro took up residence at a Capuchin monastery. He subsequently asked pardon of Maria's mother and accompanied her to Christmas Mass in the parish church. Maria Goretti's heroic story of love and forgiveness would not be complete without one of its first miraculous fruits: the conversion of Alessandro Serenelli, Maria's murderer.[1]

It's clear in Scripture and in life that when we sincerely forgive and pray for those who have hurt us (Matthew 5:44–45), it not only helps us, but it causes positive change to occur in those we forgive as well.

---

1   www.mariagoretti.org

To further stress this truth, the Lord asked me to design a cake to illustrate the paramount importance of forgiveness. Although I instantly agreed to obey the request of the Lord, I was helpless to comply without a design for the cake. I pondered for a few days as to how I should proceed, and when I wasn't successful in designing a suitable sketch, I turned the task over to the Lord. As it is written in Matthew 19:26, *"For mortals it is impossible, but for God all things are possible."*

A few days later, I was in deep prayer. In a vision, I was shown a three-tier cake covered in red icing, with gold embellishment only on the top and bottom tiers. I didn't know what the vision signified, so I asked the Lord for the purpose and meaning of this particular design. The Lord responded: You asked me for a design, and this is the design depicting "forgiveness" (cf. Matthew 7:7).

Although I was excited with God's response to my request, I was still left perplexed as to how this illustration portrayed God's message of forgiveness. Without delay, the Lord provided me with an explicit, detailed description and rationale for my vision.

The gold embellishment on the bottom tier covers and masks the red icing underneath. This symbolizes how we camouflage unforgiveness in our hearts. Our hearts may be filled with anger, resentment, bitterness, hatred, indifference, and various other negative thoughts, yet we continue in our daily lives under the false pretense that all is well.

The second tier, covered in red icing but without any ornamentation, signifies the emotional freedom we experience once we take the first step towards forgiveness—deciding to forgive, letting go of the wrongs we have experienced, and releasing from condemnation the people who have hurt us. Then our hearts feel light and unburdened; we feel free.

Forgiveness is an ongoing and layered process. Until we completely forgive from the heart, periodically a residue of anger, bitterness, resentment, and other negative feelings will resurface, depriving us of our inner peace. The gold beads on the top tier of the cake are minimal in comparison to the ornate decorations on the bottom tier. The top cake signifies the remaining negative emotions that may resurface due to incomplete forgiveness. Once we're able to fully forgive, we're no longer prisoners of our own thoughts and emotions. We have no need to masquerade or exhibit false personas.

Finally, I asked the Lord why He chose red as the base colour of the cake. His response was that red signifies sin (Ephesians 4:26–27), and unchecked unforgiveness leads to sin.

To further explain the message, the Lord drew my attention to Matthew 24:44: "*Therefore you also must be ready, for the Son of Man is coming at an unexpected hour.*" His question to all His children is: "Are you ready, truly ready, to depart from this world when the time arrives?" Are you clothed in love (Colossians 3:14), or in anger, bitterness, pride, revenge, and everything that is contrary to love (1 John 4:8)? It was a moment of epiphany for me. How ready am I? How ready are you? Do we live our lives consciously, or without mindfulness? Are we ready to depart from this world at any moment, or do we anticipate our departure to be an event in the distant future?

As mortals, we will not depart from life without hurting one another at some time, yet John 13:35 says, "*By this everyone will know that you are my disciples, if you have love for one another.*" The Lord knows our human weakness and does not expect perfection; however, He expects us to forgive each other, to pray for each other, and to reconcile with one another. By following His commandments, we demonstrate His love and His nature. God is love. When we forgive, it's to our advantage. It is written in Matthew 6:15: "*… but if you do not forgive others, neither will your Father forgive your trespasses.*" By not forgiving, we alienate ourselves from God and block ourselves from receiving His blessings and His healing.

Therefore, as children of Almighty God, we are to forgive, reconcile, and live in peace and harmony, praying for each other, as we are one body in Christ (Romans 12:5).

Bride of Christ

Let us rejoice and exult and give him the glory, for the marriage of the Lamb has come, and his bride has made herself ready. (Revelation 19:7, NRSV)

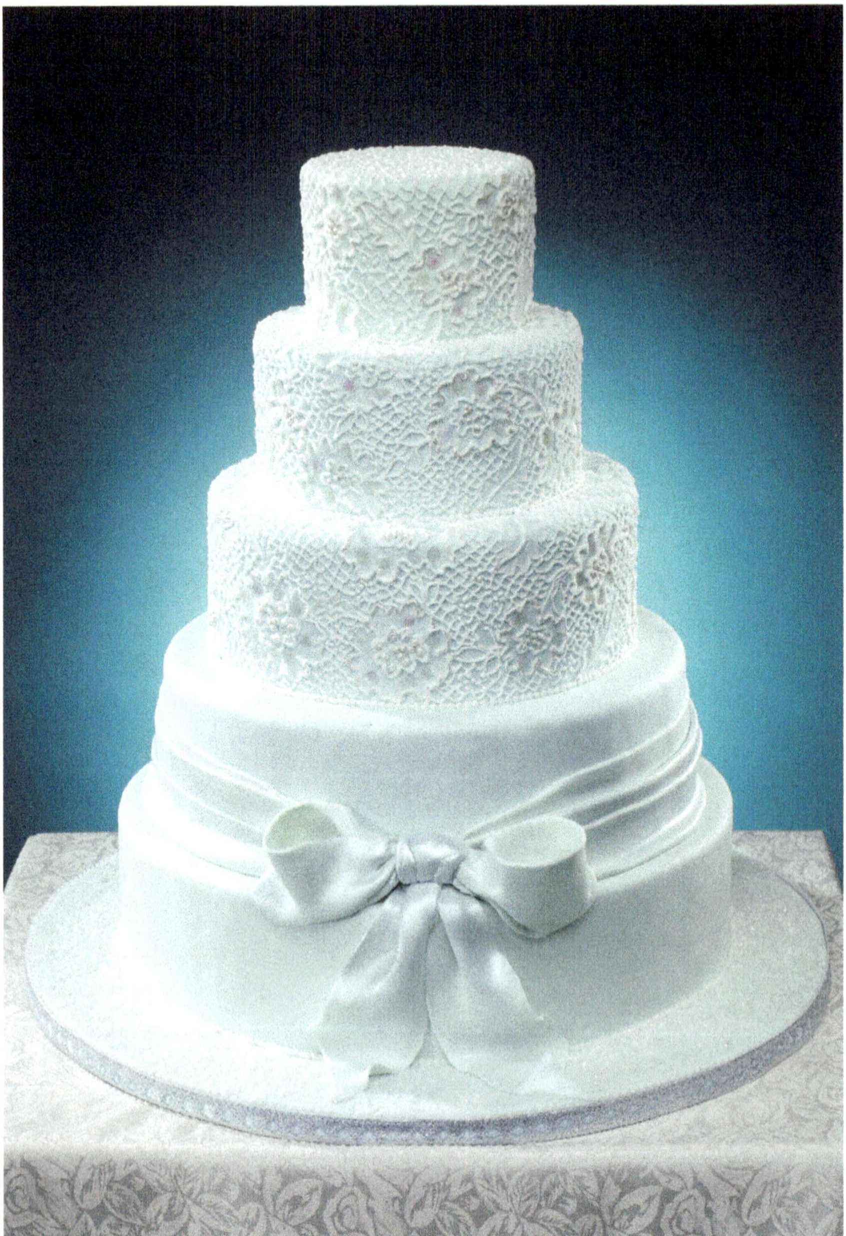

IN SCRIPTURE, OUR LORD JESUS CHRIST IS DEPICTED AS our bridegroom, and the Church as His bride. Since the church is made up of people, we are all, individually and collectively, His bride (John 3:29). Furthermore, the Lord declares, "… *for I am your husband*," (Jeremiah 3:14, NIV). Therefore, our ultimate goal in life should be to enter into an eternal marriage with our heavenly groom.

The Word of God says, "*You shall be holy, for I am holy*," (1 Peter 1:16). In order to join our groom, we need to be holy and not conform to the ways of the world (Romans 12:2). In Revelation 19:8, it is written that we are to be clothed with fine linen. Bright, beautiful, and white linen is compared to the righteous deeds of the saints. We are all called to be saints (Romans 1:7).

In a vision, to illustrate the process of transformation and purification leading to holiness, the Lord used a tiered cake as an analogy. He drew my attention toward the base tier of the cake, which is the widest of all the tiers. This is the starting point of our journey—to begin an intimate relationship with our Lord Jesus Christ, to become holy, and to enter into an eternal union with our beloved groom.

This base layer symbolizes our present state; we are sinful, broken, weak, and selfish with destructive habits and shortcomings. But when we decide to follow Jesus and welcome Him into our hearts, the Lord accepts us as we are with love and without judgment. He is joyful when one of His children decides to return to Him, much as was the father in the parable of the prodigal son (Luke 15:11–32). He ran to his wayward son, threw his arms around him, kissed him, and prepared a feast to celebrate his return home.

Next, the Lord directed my awareness to the progressively decreasing size of each tier up to the pinnacle of the cake.. This effect is achieved by either selecting smaller cake pans and reducing the cake batter, or trimming down and removing excess cake from a larger size cake.

Similarly, when we surrender our own will with an ardent desire to become holy and yield to the will of the Holy Spirit, we will be shaped and molded , according to His plan for us, as we are made in His image and likeness. As it is written, *"Yet, O Lord, you are our Father; we are the clay, and you are the potter; we are all the work of your hand,"* (Isaiah 64:8). As our characters are refined, attributes that are rooted in the secular society around us decrease and we, concurrently, increase in virtue (John 3:30).

In addition, I was shown that graduating sizes of cake tiers resemble a staircase, indicating that our journey towards holiness on Earth and in Heaven will materialize one step at a time. This change, however, can occur only with the guidance and help of the Holy Spirit. We cannot achieve this fundamental shift in personality and attitude through our own strength (John 15:5). Achieving holiness is a process. To be holy, one must enter into a personal relationship with the Lord by spending time with Him, in His Word, and by having a personal dialogue with Him, coming to know and to follow His ways.

To further illustrate the tenacity and the diligence required of us on this deep internal journey, the Lord focused my attention on the overall icing lace design of the cake. This elegant floral lace design was not achieved in a few hours or even overnight. It required numerous hours, discipline, and endurance. Each individual petal and leaf is brushed in icing with a small paint brush, and elaborate details are hand piped in icing with a piping bag. Precise measurements are required to form the icing bow. Thereafter, the entire cake is brushed with pearl sheen with a paint brush of a different width.

To produce a work of edible art, one has to master various techniques and skills, which requires dedication and continuous learning. The Lord used this cake as a comparison to emphasize the similarity between the dedication, hard work, faithfulness, endurance, and continuous learning needed to produce an artistic cake, and the qualities required to achieve our goal of transformation and purification. Though it's difficult to change our earthly lifestyle, a gradual change occurs through continuous striving, perseverance, the renunciation our worldly ways, and the embrace of a lifestyle pleasing to the Lord..

To further clarify this message regarding the process of transformation, the Lord gave me a second vision. I was shown a long, narrow, steep flight of steps, which reminded me of the image of steps illustrated by the graduated sizes of the layers of the tiered cake. The stairway consisted of many steps, almost too many to count. Looking upward from ground level, I was able to see that reaching the top of the stairway would cause great difficulty and struggle. The length of each step was approximately twelve inches long, the depth three inches (similar to the height of each cake layer—three inches); the width of the steps was very narrow. There were two walls on either side of the steps to prevent falling. I didn't comprehend the meaning of this vision.

The Lord did not keep me waiting. He immediately revealed its significance to me. It was the stairway to Heaven, a long and narrow path, a step at a time. Though climbing such a steep, narrow set of steps would be arduous and very fatiguing, if we chose to climb the staircase, we would be protected from falling off the path by the protective wall, signifying that God will protect us. I also had the sense that the walls had another purpose—to prevent us from looking either to the left or to the right, and to direct and maintain our gaze and attention towards the top of the stairs. If our gaze is fixed on Jesus, we'll accomplish our goal of reaching the top of the staircase. We'll reach Heaven and enter into an eternal marriage with our bridegroom.

It is written in Matthew 7:14: "*For the gate is narrow and the road is hard that leads to life, and there are few who find it.*" We can choose to join God in an eternal wedding banquet, or we can opt to remain on the ground in the material world while we witness others climbing the stairway toward the Lord, assuming His image and growing in holiness. It is our choice—our free will!

An Invitation

MY HOPE AND PRAYER IS THAT THIS BOOK WILL BE OF value to you, the reader, in understanding the depth of the love God has for you and of His calling to you to establish a personal relationship with Him. You are precious to Him. He is longing for you and for your response to His love.

Although God speaks to us in many ways, this book is a true testimony of God communicating with us through our daily activities. Throughout history, cakes have been symbols of celebration. Each cake featured here illustrates the central theme of the chapter.

At one time when I was saddened by the loss of a friendship, I heard the Lord say to me: "You are sad over one person, but I sacrificed my life for all my people, and most of them don't even know me. Some have even walked away from me." At one time or another, we have all experienced the pain of heartache. His heart is aching for you. He is longing for you and for your response to His love. If you focus on the crucified Jesus, His suffering and the shedding of His blood for you and me, you'll get a slight sense of His sadness and longing for you. With an aching heart He is begging to be accepted by you. Reach out to Him while you have time (Isaiah 5:6). He is reaching out to you with His arms extended.

Once you establish a relationship with Him, when trials come, as they will, you'll have Jesus to provide you with stability, strength, and guidance. Through your joys and sorrows, the Lord molds and shapes you to become His holy bride. When you are faced with difficult challenges or unpleasant circumstances, He will be beside you, even when you cannot discern or feel His presence. He will never abandon you, as that is His promise to you (Deuteronomy 31:8).

As humans we have all sinned and fallen short of the glory of God (Rom. 3:23). In the course of our lives, with those we encounter, there are bound to be misunderstandings, hurt feelings, and rejection. But as God's children we are commanded to forgive each other, to reconcile with each other, and to live in love, as God is love. Where there is love, there is God!

Seek Him while you have time (Isaiah 5:6). Experience the love of God and, respond to His calling.!

It is imperative to make God the centre of your life. Enter into a personal relationship with Him by reading His Word, spending time in personal prayer, receiving the Holy Sacraments, living His Word and by taking time in solitude and in daily conversation with the Lord. You will witness a wonderful transformation in your life. Walk with Him!

CPSIA information can be obtained
at www.ICGtesting.com
Printed in the USA
LVOW05s0750040916
503032LV00004B/4/P